Our Diwali

The Hindu Festival of Lights

It is Diwali.

Diwali is
the **Festival** of Lights.

Diwali is a time to be good and think about new beginnings.

5

Look at the lights.

We will put up the lights

for Diwali.

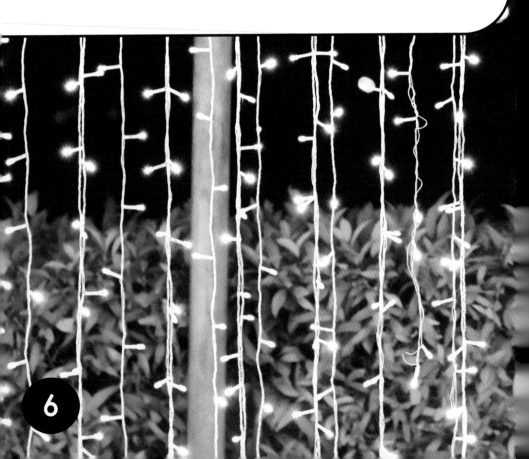

Look at my new clothes. We will buy new clothes for Diwali.

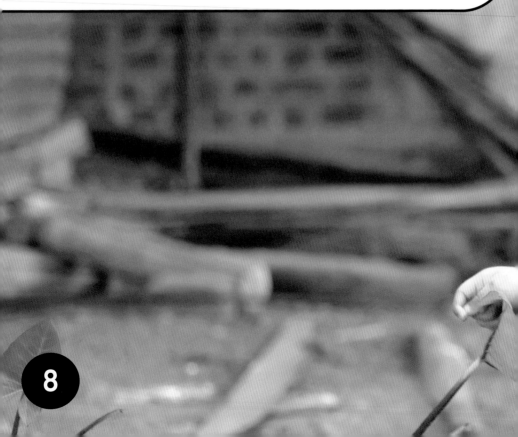

We will make **snacks** and sweets. I like eating the snacks and sweets.

We will play games.
I like playing games
with my family.

We will buy gifts
for our family.
I will give my sister a gift
for Diwali.

Glossary

festival

snacks